MISTER BOFFO
SHRINK WRAPPED

BY

JOE MARTIN

Andrews and McMeel
A Universal Press Syndicate Company
Kansas City

ISBN: 0-8362-1777-2

Library of Congress Catalog Card Number: 94-73239

ATTENTION: SCHOOLS AND BUSINESSES

Andrews and McMeel books are available at quantity discounts with bulk purchase for educational, business, or sales promotional use. For information, please write to Special Sales Department, Andrews and McMeel, 4900 Main Street, Kansas City, Missouri 64112.

8

10

14

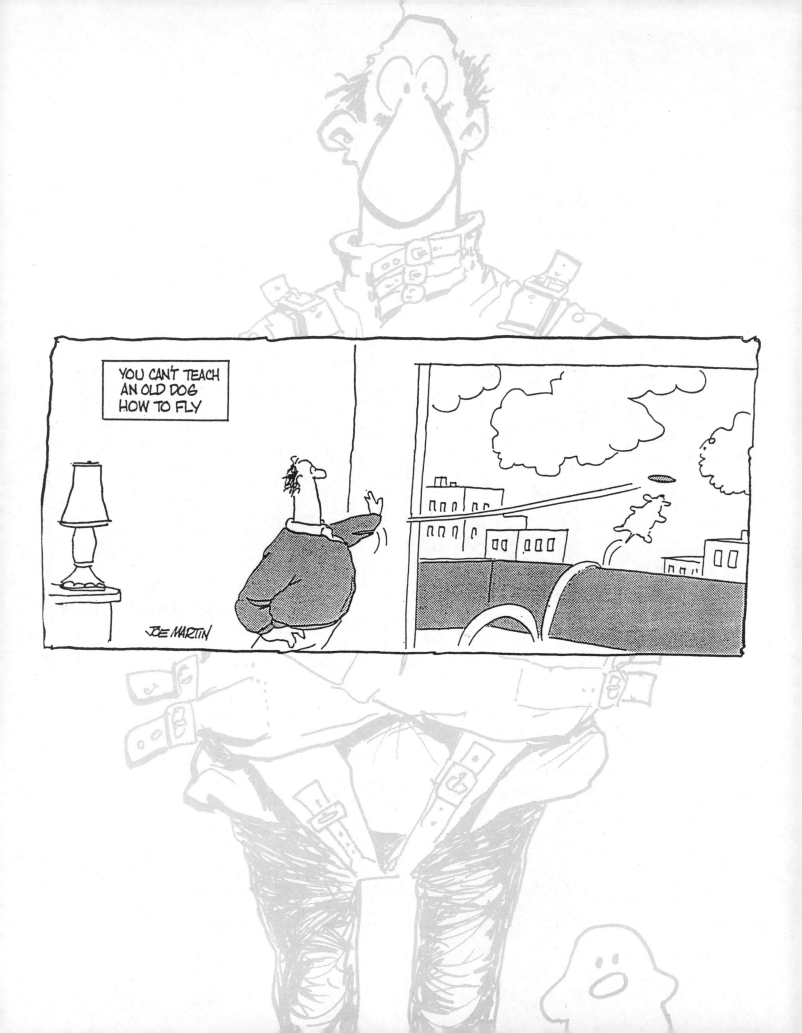

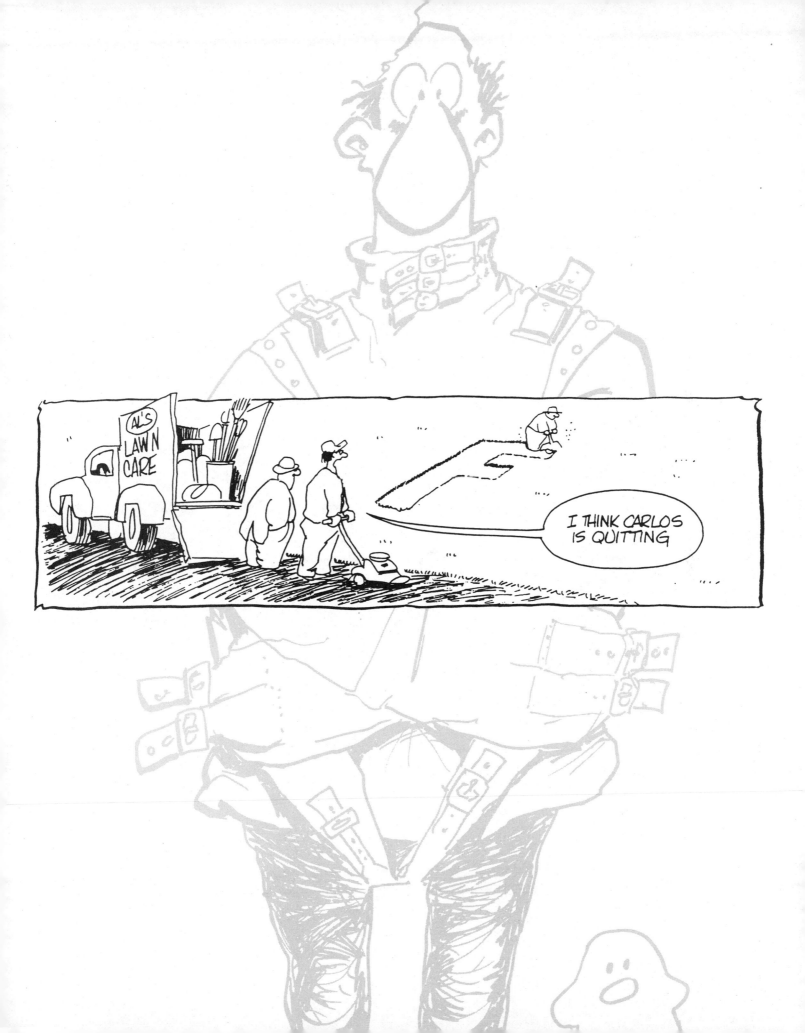

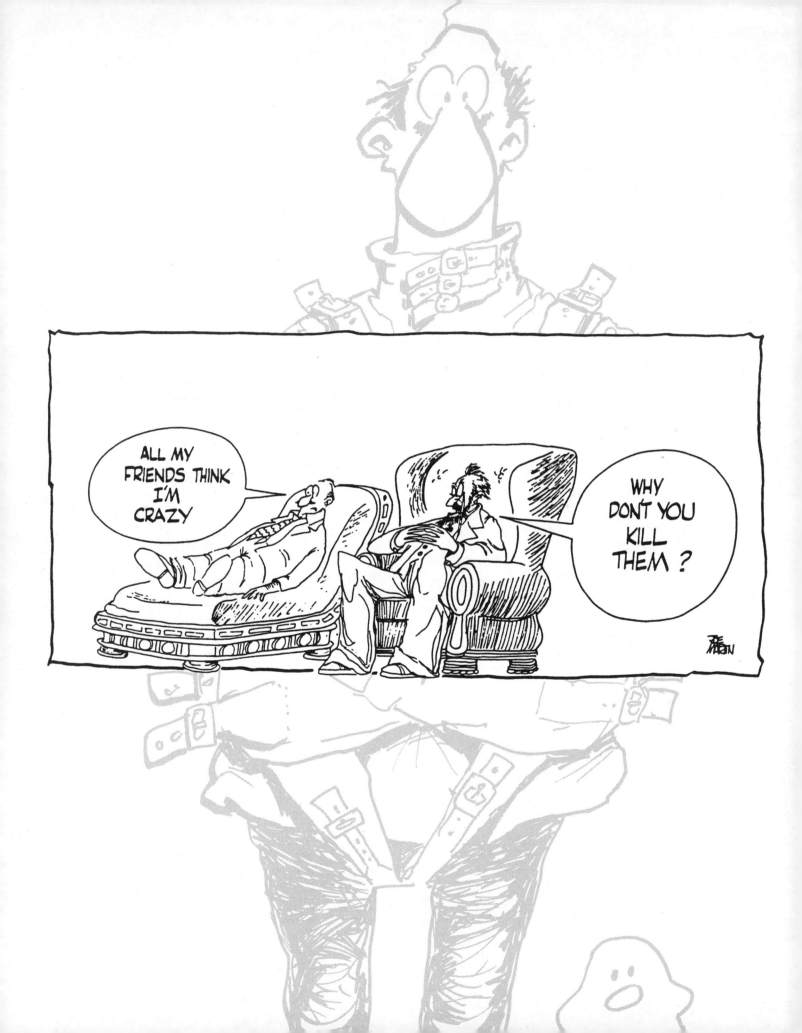

28

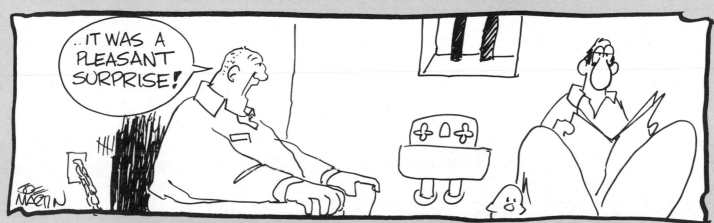

30

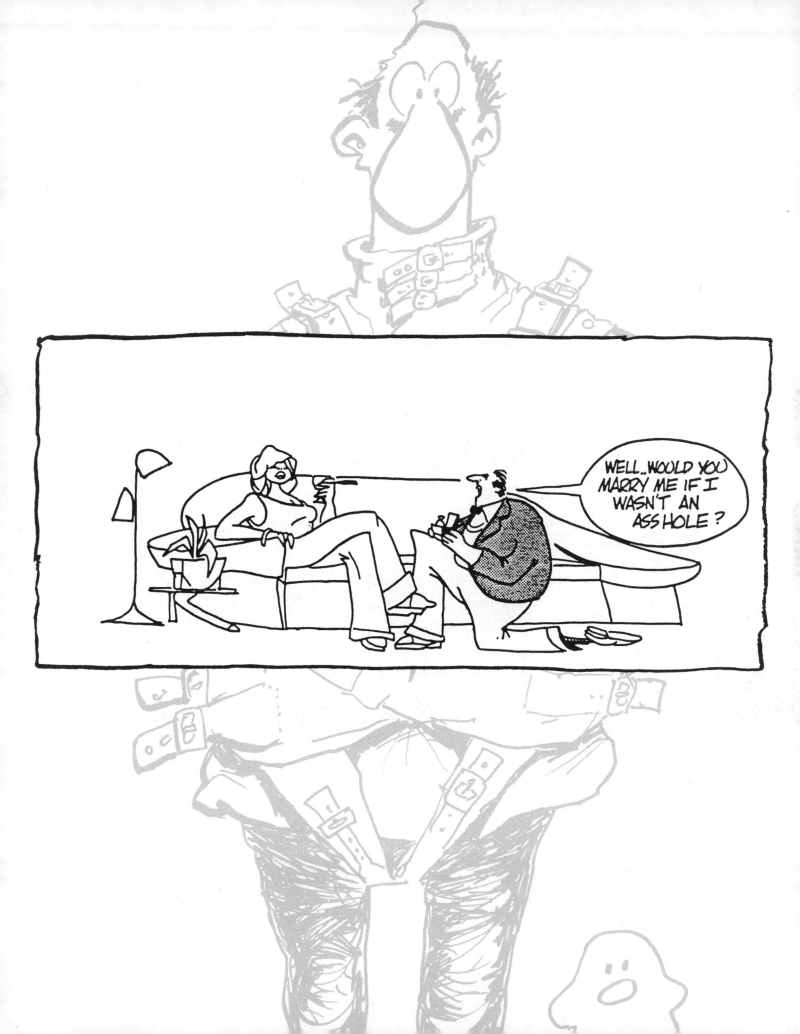

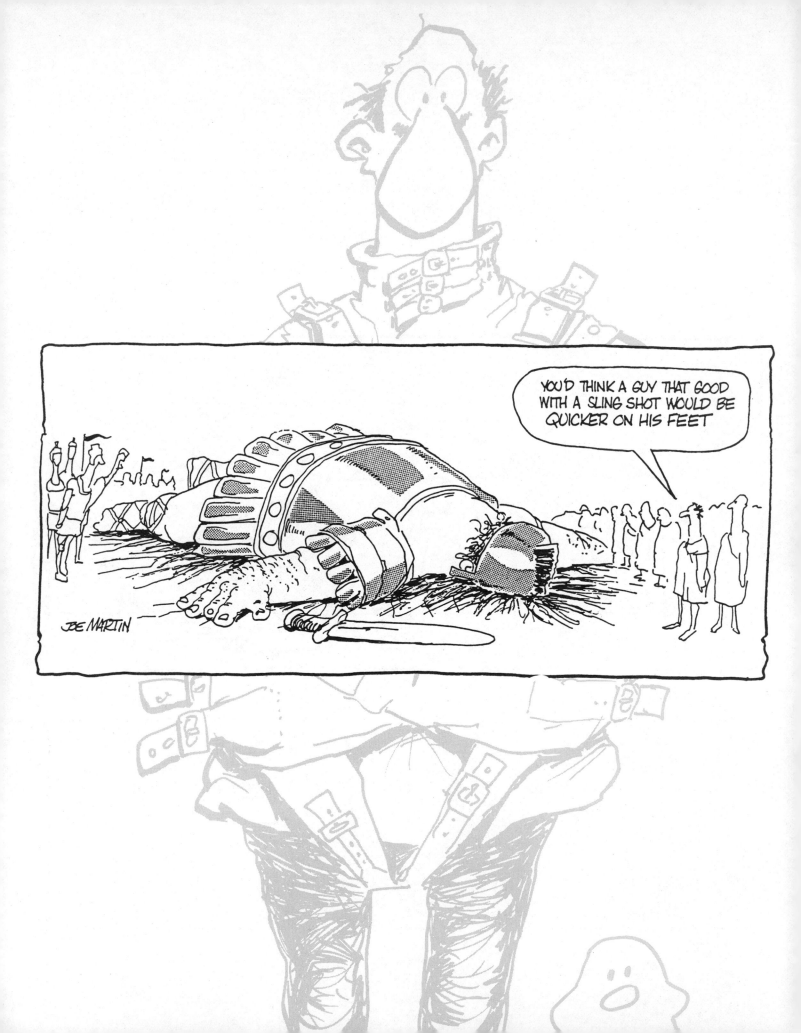

39

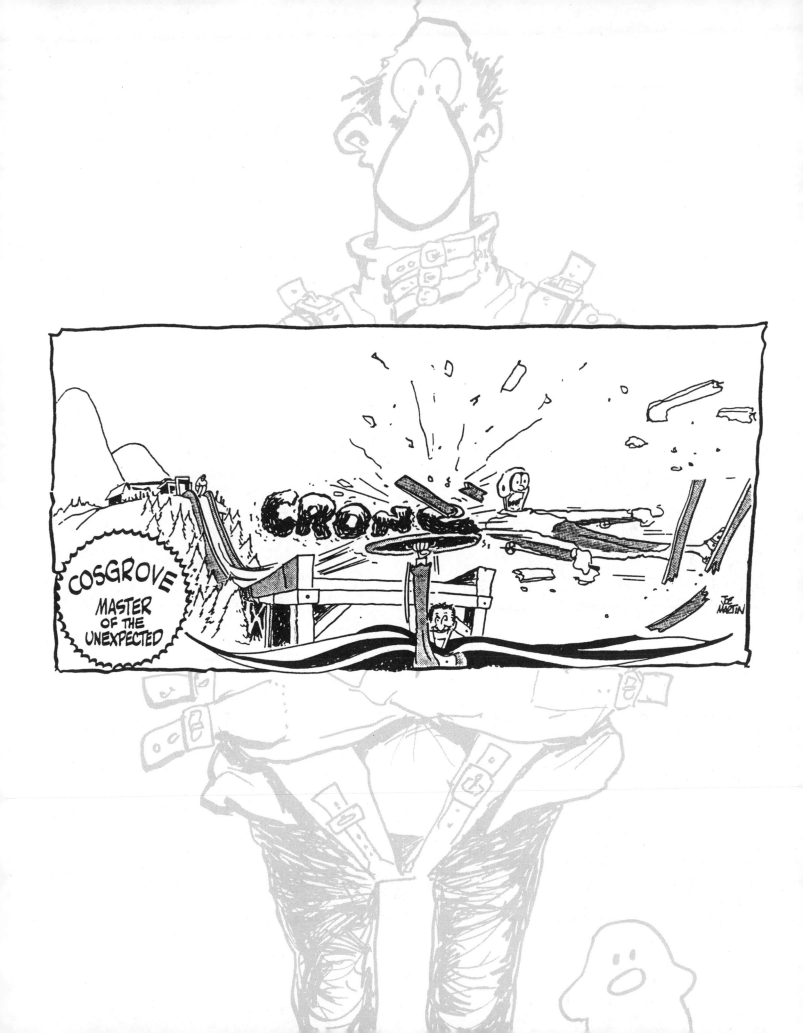

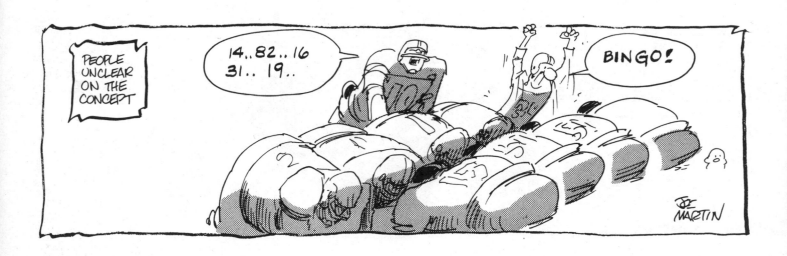

48

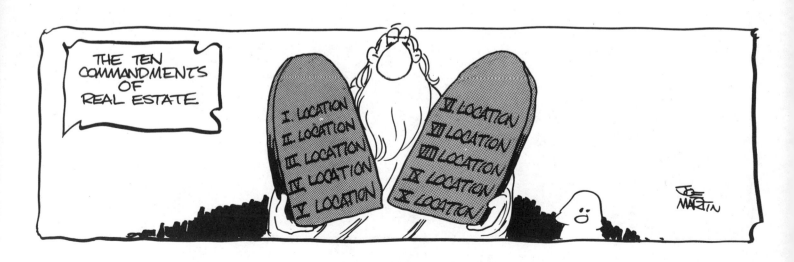

"SCHMOOZING WITH THE GUARDS"

...THE THING PRISONERS MISS MOST WHILE IN SOLITAIRE—

AND HIS WONDER-DOG "WEEDERMAN"
BY JOE MARTIN

AN OPEN LETTER TO READERS: FOR THE PAST 5 YEARS I'VE BEEN DESCRIBED AS A GHOST, A DOODLE, A BALL, A PUFF, A TUFT... A BLOB AND, MOST RECENTLY, A FLUFFY PIECE OF TOAST!...

ALL THIS TIME I STOOD BY, STARING INTO SPACE, WHILE THIS "BOFFO" CHARACTER HAMS IT UP!! WELL, WEEDERMAN THE WONDER DOG'S LIPS ARE NO LONGER SEALED!

THE WHOLE SORDID "BEHIND-THE-SCENES" STORY IS TOLD IN MY UPCOMING WEEDERMAN NEWSLETTER, "BOFFO DEAREST!"

SEND NOW FOR THE FIRST ISSUE, WHICH ALSO DEALS WITH... SLEAZY TABLOIDS!...THE CLODS THAT RUN THEM, AND HOW THEY WOULDN'T KNOW A GOOD STORY IF IT BIT 'EM!

WEEDERMAN NEWSLETTER
C/O JOE MARTIN
P.O. BOX 86 C
LAKE GENEVA, WI.
53147

AND A WEEDERMAN* POSTER

*AND BOFFO

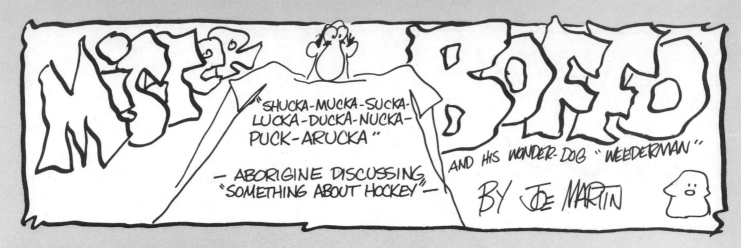

58

70

A BIG PART OF THE REASON DISNEY NEVER MADE IT AS A PORTRAIT ARTIST

SPEED BUMP FROM HELL

A TIME TO WORRY

NOW IS A GOOD TIME TO HAVE THE OPERATION ... HIS RATES ARE MUCH CHEAPER WHILE HE'S COMPLETING HIS COMMUNITY SERVICE HOURS.

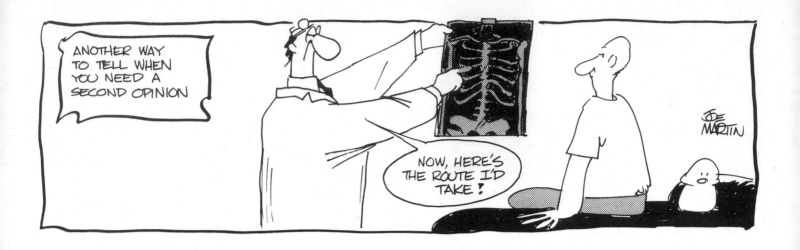

75

80

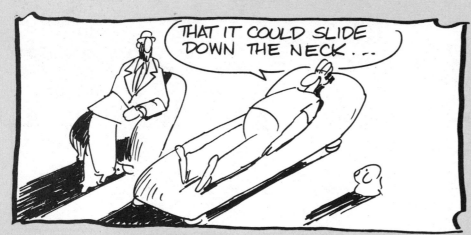

84

85

95

COMPUTER FIGHT VIDEO: DEMPSEY VS. THE INVISIBLE MAN

INTERNAL REVENUE SERVICE

AUDIT DIV.

HERE'S HOW WE'LL WORK IT... YOU PICK THE FIGURE YOU THINK YOU SHOULD PAY, AND I'LL PICK THE FIGURE WE'LL MULTIPLY IT BY...

LEAST SUCCESSFUL APPLICATION OF THE HONOR SYSTEM

"CHECK BOX 'A' IF YOU THINK YOU SHOULD BE AUDITED"

118

DOOFUS ROULETTE

THE SINGLE BIGGEST REASON WHY THERE ARE NO WINDOWS IN OPERATING ROOMS OF HOSPITALS BUILT ON OR NEAR PARADE ROUTES

129

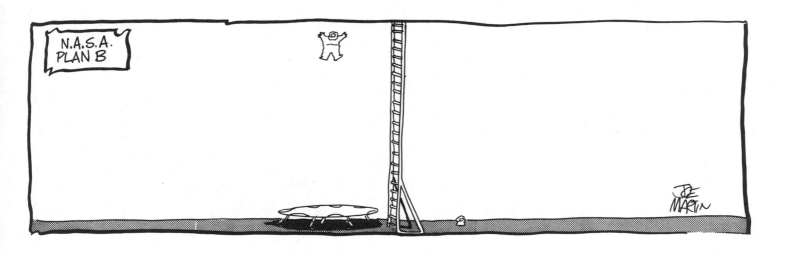

141

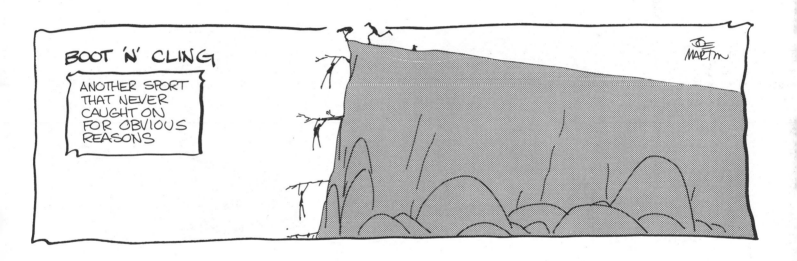

159

160

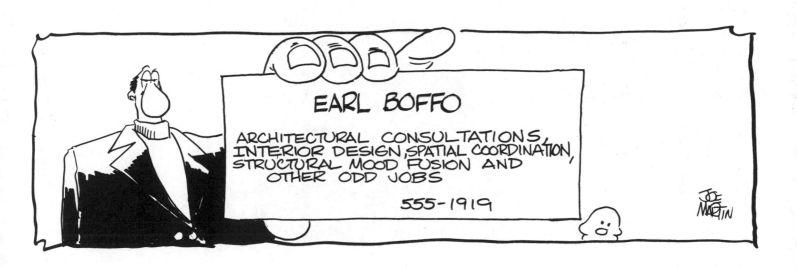

169

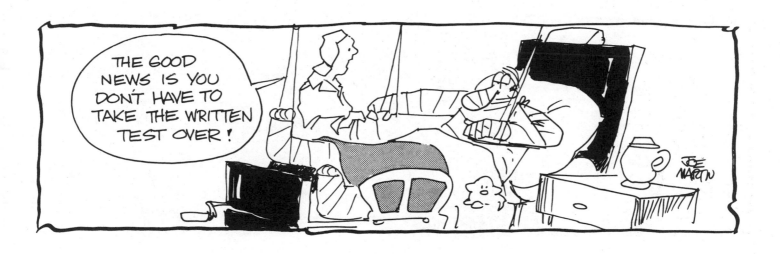

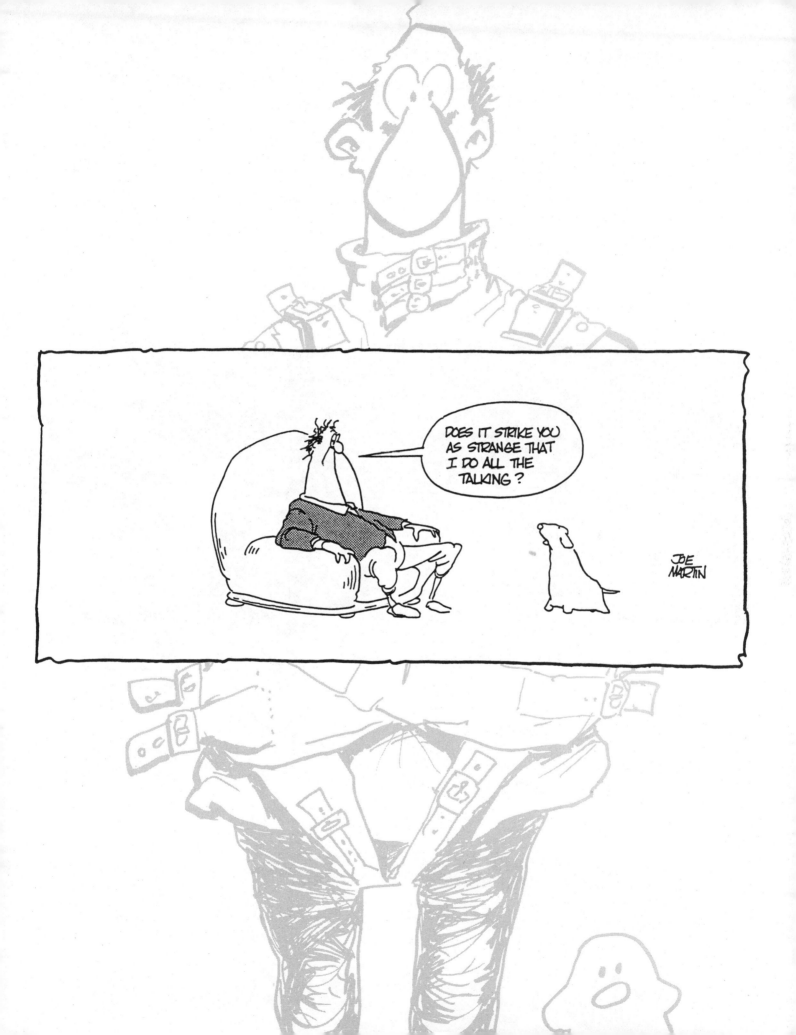

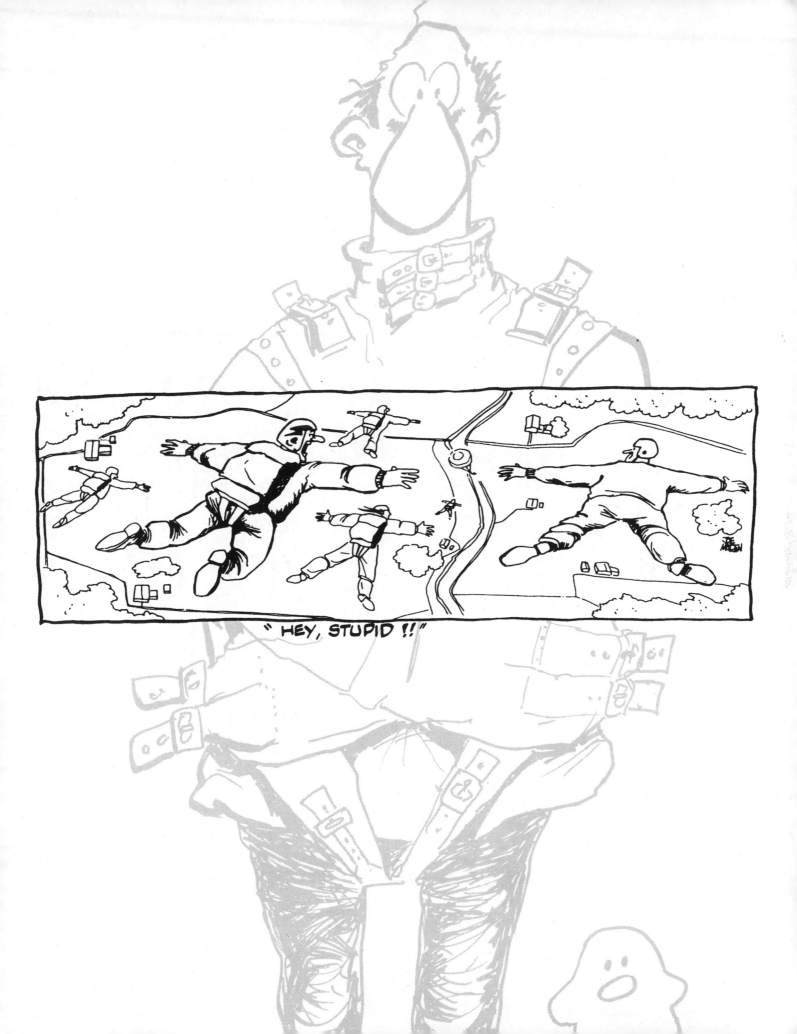

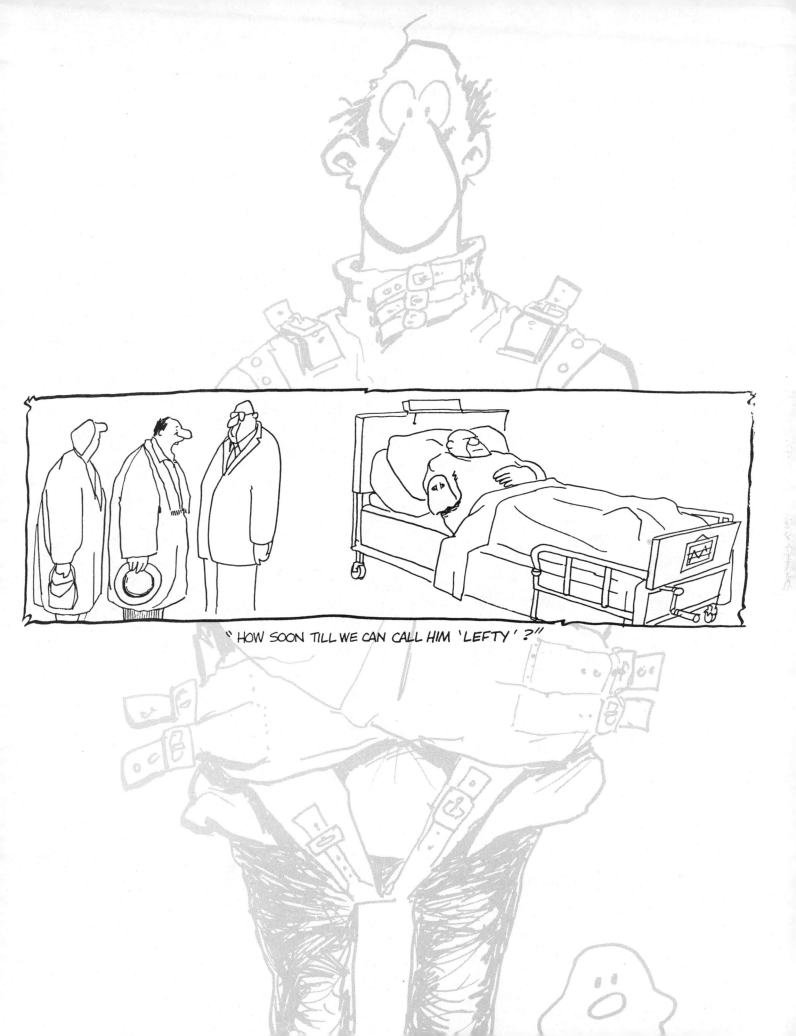

"HOW SOON TILL WE CAN CALL HIM 'LEFTY'?"

MISTER BOFFO

"WHATEVER"

— NUMBER ONE ON LIST OF SNAPPY COMEBACKS IN THE LAND OF THE TINY-BRAINED FOLK —

AND HIS WONDER-DOG "WEEDERMAN"

BY JOE MARTIN

CALL ME "TUBES", I'VE HAD THE NICKNAME ALL MY LIFE. GOT IT BECAUSE I BRUSH MY TEETH SO MUCH ...

I BRUSH TWICE IN THE MORNING, TWICE AT NIGHT, THREE TIMES AFTER EACH MEAL! AND MANY TIMES JUST FOR FUN.!...I'M NEVER WITHOUT MY TUBE OF TOOTHPASTE!

EVERY MORNING WHEN I WAS A KID I'D STUFF MY POCKETS WITH TOOTHPASTE. ONE DAY A PAL YELLS OUT, "HEY, TUBES" AND IT STUCK!

IT'S "TUBS" NOT "TUBES" AND IT'S BECAUSE HE EATS LIKE A PIG!... ALTHOUGH SOME PEOPLE CALL HIM "MISTER LOUD" BECAUSE HE'S ALSO HALF-DEAF.

JOE MARTIN